Angel's Brave New Beginning

A True Story

Written and Visualized by John Good

This story is based on true events. Some details have been gently adapted for young readers.

Special Thanks

With gratitude to the kind hearts who helped Angel find her way, to the caregivers who showed her patience and love, and to every rescue dog who reminds us that hope can begin anywhere.

For Maddie

The angel who brought us Angel

"Dogs come into our lives to teach us
about love; they depart to teach us
about loss.

A new dog never replaces an old dog;
it merely expands the heart.

If you have loved many dogs
your heart is very big."

— *Erica Jong*

Once upon a time, in a place where the *waves whispered to the sand* and *the gulls called to the sky*, there stood a husky named Angel.

She didn't have a home, and the beach felt bigger and lonelier than anything she had known before. She did not know where she belonged, or where she was going-only that her heart hoped for something better.

And though she didn't yet know it,
her story was about to change
in the most magical way.

Angel wandered the misty beaches for what must have felt like forever. It was cold, windy, and the rain fell sideways so every inch of her was soaked to the bone. Her fur was matted from wind and seawater, and a tattered rope still hung from her neck.

She kept far away from people,
watching them with cautious, tired eyes.
She only had bad memories of people.
She didn't feel safe.

"I want help," she often thought,
"But I don't know if I can trust anyone..."

One morning, a man driving along
the shoreline spotted her.
Angel froze when he slowed down
to look at her.

"Please don't come closer," she thought anxiously. But he didn't chase her or call loudly, he simply watched with gentle concern
before driving away to tell others.

Soon, word spread through the community, and many people came to help. They set out bowls of food and fresh water.

They spoke softly and moved slowly,
hoping Angel would feel safe.
But fear held her paws firmly in place.

That night, the man saw Angel on the beach.

She was alone.

This made the man sad.

He hoped she would be safe.

The next day, Angel was able to free herself from the rope that was around her neck. She felt free. She felt safer than she had before. She was happier.

The people who came to help would bring their dogs to the beach, and Angel would play with them joyfully. She loved having other dogs as friends.

The man in the white car
came to the beach every day.
He kept a close watch on Angel's every move,
following her up and down the beach.
He wanted to make sure she was safe.

Angel was still afraid to be close to people.
There was something that kept her away.
The people seemed nice.
She just couldn't trust them.

One afternoon, a kind trapper in
a bright red van arrived.
She spoke in gentle tones, moved
with calm patience, and set a safe trap
with food meant only to help.

The scent of fresh food drifted through the breeze. Angel sniffed it, hesitating. "I'm hungry... maybe this is okay," she thought. Still, she waited with caution.

By late afternoon, hunger was stronger than fear. She stepped inside. She tasted the gift of a meal. The trap door closed. She was safe.

The trapper brought Angel to the veterinarian, where the kind man was waiting.

They brought her inside where Angel
experienced the comfort
of being warm and dry.
Maybe it was for the first time.

At the vet, everything felt unfamiliar. New smells. New sounds. Angel curled in her kennel, thinking, "Where am I? Am I really safe?"

That night, Angel slept the soundest sleep she ever had.
She was warm.
She was safe.

Angel woke up the next morning
and most of her fur was shaved away.
The doctor had to shave her because
it was so matted and dirty.
She was cold, but she felt much better.

Later that day, the kind man arrived.
He saw that she was cold.
He put a blanket on her for warmth.
Angel looked at him with grateful eyes.

The man visited her every single day.
He would sit beside her
so she wouldn't feel alone.
He brought treats, spoke in soft,
patient tones, and let her choose
when to come closer.

Day by day, she grew braver.
She inched closer and closer.
She began to believe
that this man was different.
Someone she could trust.

The more the man came to see her,
the more Angel would think,
"Why does he care?
Why does he keep coming back?
Why does his voice make
my heart feel calmer?"

On a sunny day, the man and a trainer
helped Angel go outside.
She felt the warm sun on her face.
She was happy and calm.

The day for Angel to come home
had arrived.
That morning, a rainbow appeared,
with reassurance from an old friend.
The man knew it would be a good day.

At the vet, the man asked,
"Are you ready to come home, sweet girl?"
Angel didn't know the word "home,"
but she understood the feeling in his voice.

Angel was ready.
She climbed into the kennel
for the car ride.
She wanted so much to learn more
about this place called "home".

When Angel arrived at her new home, she was filled with hope and curiosity. Her eyes grew wide and her heart raced with excitement at what she saw.

Sitting in the grass were two large
Great Pyrenees dogs.
Their faces were full of welcoming
happiness and joy.
Their names were Sookie and Charlie.

Sookie, the girl, approached Angel first.
Angel trembled.
"Will she be kind to me?"

Sookie sniffed her gently, then stood beside her like a snowy guardian. It was her way of saying, "You're safe. I'm here for you."

Angel then met Charlie. She gently touched his nose. Charlie gave her a big smile. Angel thought to herself, "Are you my new big brother?"

That night, Angel slept soundly
in her kennel. Sookie, her protector,
watched over her new friend.

Angel slept better that night than she ever had. She was warm. She was happy. She was safe.

The next morning, Angel was ready to see more things. She came out of her kennel, eager to see what the day would bring.

Angel went outside and looked around the yard. Her heart was filling with happiness. She was so happy, she had to let out a big....

HOWWWWOOOOOOOOL!

Sookie and Charlie heard Angel's happy howl.
They smiled the biggest smiles.
They knew their new
family member was happy.

Angel saw Sookie and Charlie's smiles.
She leaned down into her play stance.
Then, something exciting happened...

It was ***PLAYTIME!***

Angel had never had a brother and sister to play with. Being with Sookie and Charlie made her very happy.

For a few nights, Angel slept inside her kennel. It was the only space where she felt safe. But every night, Sookie curled up nearby, offering comfort with her steady presence.

It didn't take long for Angel to sleep outside of her kennel. She would curl up close with Sookie for big fluffy naps.

Angel started taking peaceful naps on rugs, blankets, and cozy spots around the home, always choosing to be near her new sister.

Sometimes Angel and Charlie would relax together too.
Angel always loved her Charlie time.

Every day, Angel, Sookie, and Charlie would happily spend time in the yard together.

As Angel blossomed, her family felt their own hearts grow warmer.

From that moment on, every moment
became special.
The first time she rolled on her back to play...

The first time she surfed the counter...

The first time she discovered the joys
of digging in the dirt...

The first time Sookie chased
her around the yard...

The first time she playfully
nudged Charlie...

And the first time Charlie invited Angel to nap with him...

Each moment filled her family with joy,
a deep, glowing, and grateful joy.

The more she trusted, the more their love for her grew. And the more they loved her, the braver she became.

Before long, Angel felt truly at home.

She zoomed joyfully around the yard,
happy energy bursting from her paws.

She wrestled with Sookie and Charlie,
rolling and tumbling in laughter.

She learned that hands could be gentle...

Food came from bowls at dinnertime...

... And that love could surround her like sunshine.

Angel wasn't the frightened husky
on the beach anymore.

She was loved, and Angel thought to herself...
"Maybe I really do belong here."

She was safe. She was home.
She had a loving family.

Angel learned that family isn't just
who you're born with.
Family is who comes together to rescue you,
heal you, and love you forever.

Angel, Sookie, and Charlie today.

Some stories begin with courage.

The best ones end with family.

www.ingramcontent.com/pod-product-compliance
Ingram Content Group UK Ltd.
Pitfield, Milton Keynes, MK11 3LW, UK
UKHW060401300726
14090UKWH00001B/52

* 9 7 9 8 9 9 4 9 5 6 1 1 3 *